THE
LOST CITY OF
ATLANTIS

BY
HARRIETTE ABELS

EDITED BY
Dr. Howard Schroeder
Professor in Reading and Language Arts
Dept. of Curriculum and Instruction
Mankato State University

PUBLISHED BY
CRESTWOOD HOUSE

CIP

LIBRARY OF CONGRESS CATALOGING IN PUBLICATION DATA

Abels, Harriette Sheffer.
  Lost city of Atlantis.

  (The Mystery of ——)
  SUMMARY: Explores the possibility that the ancient continent of Atlantis may
have actually existed.
  1. Atlantis—Juvenile literature. [1. Atlantis] I. Schroeder, Howard. II. Title.
III. Series.
GN751.A34   1987   398.2'34   87-13440
ISBN 0-89686-344-1

International Standard Book Number:	Library of Congress Catalog Card Number:
0-89686-344-1	87-13440

CREDITS

Illustrations:
Library of Congress: 5, 7
Nancy DeVore/Anthro-Photo File: 9
Marvin Davis/Portuguese National Tourist Office: 10-11, 42-43
Milwaukee Public Museum: 12-13
Bob Williams: 15, 16, 22, 24-25, 31, 38-39, 40-41
UPI/Bettmann Newsphotos: 18
Bahamas Ministry of Tourism: 20, 26-27
Springer/Bettmann Film Archive: 28-29
James W. Mavor, Jr.: 32, 33, 34-35, 36
Andy Schlabach: 44-45, 46
Graphic Design & Production:
Baker Street Productions, Ltd.

CRESTWOOD·HOUSE

Box 3427, Mankato, MN, U.S.A. 56002

MEDIALOG
Alexandria, Ky 41001

2/88

THE LOST CITY OF ATLANTIS

TABLE OF CONTENTS

Chapter 1

Once there was a land of golden cities with great ports and huge temples. Tall, beautiful trees grew all around. Fountains bubbled with both hot and cold water. Mountains surrounded the royal city, and rivers, lakes and meadows supplied enough food for every living creature. This lovely land was called Atlantis.

But was Atlantis real, or only a myth? Did Atlantis ever exist, or was it simply the product of an ancient culture's imagination?

Plato was a Greek philosopher who lived in the fourth century B.C. He wrote about Atlantis in two dialogues, *Timaeus* and *Critias*. Dialogues are compositions in which two or more characters carry on a conversation. During Plato's time, dialogues were a common form for telling tales of ancient history.

Plato's story of Atlantis was a startling account of a continent that sank into the sea. According to the original story, Atlantis was a powerful empire existing more than nine thousand years before Plato's time. It came to a sudden end while going to war, probably with prehistoric Greece. Plato says the central island or islands sank under the Atlantic Ocean "in a terrible night and day." Since that time it has lain on the bottom

The Greek philosopher, Plato, was the first person to write about Atlantis.

of the ocean, lost forever.

When Plato first wrote the story of Atlantis, people believed it was true. Since that time, over 25,000 books have been written on the subject. Today, few modern scholars believe Atlantis ever existed. But there are some who believe it did.

It is believed that Christopher Columbus had heard about Atlantis before he made his first voyage. Greek documents and accurate maps of the Atlantic Ocean had spread across Europe by that time. Columbus is thought to have seen an early copy of a Greek map which clearly showed the eastern coast of South America, although that continent supposedly had not yet been discovered. Columbus' son, Fernando, reported that his father was very interested in reports of sunken lands under the ocean. In fact, the place in the Bahamas where Columbus made his first landfall was a high point of an underwater mass of land.

As the Spanish continued their exploration of the New World, they found that the Indians of Mexico and Central America had many words that sounded like "Atlantis." These words were names for the place the Indians had come from, many years earlier.

The Indians also had other legends which were similar to our biblical stories. They told of a great flood and people who survived on ships with their animals. They also told of building a huge tower to escape the next flood.

But strangest of all was the Indian's belief that the Spaniards were the ancient white gods who, centuries before, had brought them civilization. It is strange, indeed, that the Spanish conquerors were hoping to find Atlantis, while the American Indian races expected the return of their gods. Because of this, it was much easier for a small number of Spaniards to conquer the huge Indian tribes.

The Aztec emperor, Montezuma, welcomes Spanish explorer Hernan Cortes.

Chapter 2

The name Atlantis comes to us from the ancient Greek language. The Greeks called the tribes on the northwest coast of Africa *Atalantes* or *Atarantes*. The Greeks believed these people were refugees from the Atlantis tragedy.

There are many reasons to believe that at one time a place like Atlantis really did exist. Some scientists believe there is truth in the story because names similar to Atlantis appear in several areas.

First, of course, is the Atlantic Ocean. Plato said that Atlantis was not in the Mediterranean Ocean, but far out in the Atlantic beyond the "Pillars of Hercules." That is what the ancient peoples called the area between Gibraltar, on the southern coast of Spain, and Mount Atlas on the northern shore of Africa.

The Berber tribes of North Africa have a legend about a country they call Attala. This was a war-like kingdom off the African coast. It was rich in gold, silver and tin. The Berber tale says that Attala is now under the ocean, but will one day reappear.

In ancient Gaul, Ireland and Wales, people believed that their ancestors came from a continent that sank into the western sea. The Welsh and the British called this place "the lost paradise of Avalon." Avalon appears in the ancient tales of King Arthur and his court.

There is an area in southern France and northern Spain called the Basque country. The people who live there speak a language unlike any other language in Europe. It bears no relation to either the French or the Spanish languages. A tradition among the Basque people says that they came from "somewhere else." They believe their people are from a country they call Atlaintika.

The Portuguese believe that Atlantis was near Portugal and that the Azores Islands are actually the

Members of the Berber tribe tell of a land called "Attala," which they believe lies beneath the sea.

tops of mountains in ancient Atlantis.

The Spanish believe the same about the Canary Islands. When Spain first conquered the Canary Islands, the natives claimed to be the only survivors of a world-wide disaster.

The ancient Vikings thought that Atli was a marvelous land in the west. It is also thought that sailors from Venice and Carthage, too, knew of a thriving western island which they called Antilla. They tried to keep their knowledge about Antilla secret so that other nations would not interfere with their commerce and colonization of the island.

Some people think that the Azores Islands near Portugal were actually mountain tops in Atlantis. Shown above is Mount Pico.

Ancient Egyptian hieroglyphics talk about Amenti, the paradise of the west. The Babylonians called their western paradise Arallu, while the ancient Arabians thought civilization first began in the land of Ad, which was located somewhere in the western ocean.

When the Spanish conquerors first went north from Central and South America into Mexico, they found that the Aztecs had similar ideas. The Aztecs believed that their ancestors had originally come from an island in the ocean east of them (the Atlantic Ocean) called Aztlan. The conquerors also found a settlement in Venezuela called Atlan, and they called the people there

Early explorers of North America found an ancient village in the state of Wisconsin that the local Indians called Aztalan.

"white Indians."

There were also legends among the North American Indian tribes that said their ancestors had come from an island in the Atlantic. Early explorers of our state of Wisconsin found a fortified village near Lake Michigan that the Indians called Aztalan.

All of these similar names do not prove that the continent of Atlantis did exist, but they do prove that Plato did not simply invent the story of Atlantis. Some

of these legends, and the ancient names, were passed
down from a time thousands of years before Plato. They
come from parts of the world that had no communica-
tion with each other.

There are legends even among the people of the
Pacific Islands, which tell of the sinking of great land
masses in that area. They tell of the earth shaking and
islands disappearing into the ocean. It is these stories
of ''land disappearing'' that keep the Atlantis legend
alive.

Chapter 3

According to Plato, the story of Atlantis was first told by Egyptian priests to Solon, a great Athenian law-maker, around the sixth century B.C. Solon told the story to a relative, who told it to his son, and that son to his son. Finally, it was told to a man named Critias who was an Athenian statesman living at the same time as Plato.

Plato described Atlantis in detail. He spoke of a royal city, with bridges and roads leading to a royal palace. A beautiful canal led from the sea to the harbor. It was three hundred feet (91 m) wide and one hundred feet (30 m) deep. The stone used to build the canal was quarried from under the center of the island. There were red, black and white stones.

A wall surrounded the outer city. It was covered with a coating of brass. An inner wall was coated with tin, and a third, smaller wall with a metal called orichalcun. This was a yellow metal considered precious by the ancient Greeks. It was probably a type of brass.

Plato's description of the palaces and temples is magnificent. He talked of fountains with cold and hot water. The people of Atlantis also made cisterns, some with open roofs, that were used in the wintertime as warm baths. There were special baths for the king and others for private citizens. There were separate baths for women and others for horses and cattle.

Beautiful trees of great height grew all around. Temples were built and dedicated to many gods. Some gardens were set aside as places of exercise. These were not only for people, but also for horses. In the center of one of the two large islands was a race track.

Once out of the city, there was a large level plain surrounded by mountains. The mountains were huge and beautiful. There were many wealthy villages of country people. Rivers, lakes and meadows supplied

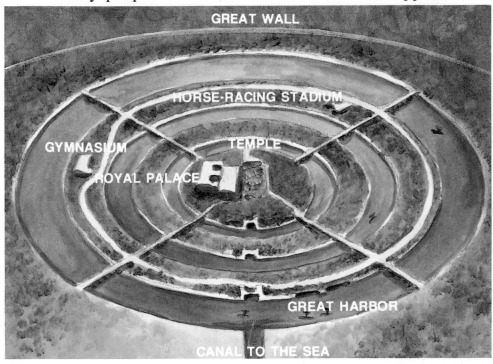

This illustration of the city of Atlantis is based on Plato's detailed description.

Civilization in Atlantis progressed rapidly.

enough food for all the animals, wild or tame.

Plato described a huge population. He said Atlantis had trained armed forces, with ten thousand chariots and twelve hundred ships. Atlantis' armies planned to subdue all Mediterranean countries, and they were successful in parts of Europe and Africa. But the Greek city-state of Athens resisted their attack and later defeated Atlantis' military forces.

Chapter 4

Edgar Cayce was a famous American psychic. He was called "the sleeping prophet." Cayce was a simple, ordinary man—except when he was in a psychic trance. While in a trance, he was able to give detailed medical readings for people around the world who were ill. Although he is known mainly for his medical readings, Cayce also did readings on other subjects.

Cayce first mentioned Atlantis in a reading he gave in 1923. He thought that the first portions of Atlantis would rise again in 1968 or 1969. He also said that part of an Atlantean temple would be discovered near the island of Bimini, off the coast of Florida. Because of this prophesy, many famous pilots began to watch the Bimini Banks as they flew over them. In 1969, undersea explorers reported many new underwater sightings, and a number of important stone areas were found.

Cayce gave a detailed description of what life was like in Atlantis before it was destroyed. Of course, we have no way of knowing if anything Cayce said was true, but many of his readings and predictions on other subjects have been true. Perhaps his picture of Atlantis is also close to the truth.

He described Atlantis as an important land area. It

Psychic Edgar Cayce gave his view of life in Atlantis in a 1923 reading.

occupied what was later the North Atlantic Ocean. The eastern coast of the United States was then mostly under water. The coastal lowlands of Atlantis extended from the Gulf of Mexico to the Mediterranean Sea. Bimini, the Bahamas, the British West Indies and southern Mexico were all part of the continent of Atlantis, Cayce said.

Civilization progressed rapidly in Atlantis, far more rapidly than on the other continents. In an early period, Atlanteans lived in houses of wood. Next came circular houses of stone. Once they were hunters. Then they became herders and farmers, and used stone and wood tools. They discovered fire and natural gas. Then they discovered iron and copper. They made balloons from the hides of elephants and other large animals, and also used the hides to make buildings. Huge beasts roamed the forests of the mountains and the jungles of the valleys. Giant fowl hovered above the earth.

Beautiful stone cities were scattered across the land. Water was supplied to the buildings from nearby mountain streams. Each city was centered around a temple with a sacred fire burning at the altar. In the temples were also large rooms for the priests and priestesses, who acted as judges as well as spiritual leaders. This was true of many ancient religions.

The Atlanteans were originally a peaceful nation, eager to obey the laws of nature. Over the centuries, however, the people misused the forces of nature. Finally, Cayce said, violence and trouble spread across the land. And then came great natural disasters. Giant upheavals shook the earth. Islands crumbled into the sea and disappeared beneath the waters. Only the scat-

Edgar Cayce predicted that the remains of an Atlantean temple would be discovered near this island, called Bimini.

tered mountain peaks were left.

Some people escaped the tragedy, but most were lost. By 9500 B.C., Atlantis had vanished from the earth. But the culture that had developed over thousands of centuries did not completely disappear. Atlantis had been in contact with other peoples and had shared some of its knowledge. And those fortunate enough to escape took their culture with them.

Chapter 5

In the past twenty years there have been a number of scientific searches to find the location of the lost continent. There is one problem that hinders their search: No one really knows where the continent of Atlantis was. On both sides of the Atlantic Ocean are massive, unexplained underwater ruins. We do not know who built them. The most interesting thing about these ruins is that the builders must have used certain techniques and devices thousands of years before these things were thought to be invented.

Huge stone ruins have been photographed and explored off the coasts of North Africa, Mexico, South America and the Bahamas. Other ruins have been investigated off the coasts of Spain, Portugal, the Azores Islands, Canary Islands and northern Africa. Many of these ruins resemble each other. They also resemble ancient ruins in South America, Asia and the Pacific islands.

Did all of these mysterious ruins come from an ancient Atlantean culture?

There is some evidence of a connection between Atlantis and the mysterious Bermuda Triangle. Strange formations have been seen in the shallow sea off the

In the above picture, a diver searches among ancient ruins for a clue to the mystery of Atlantis.

Bermuda Banks. Airline pilots, flying at low altitudes, have said that some of these formations look like the tops of buildings sunk under the floor of the sea.

It is much harder to see these formations from sea level than it is from the air. For years these were thought to be either natural formations or the remains of ship-wrecks. For centuries, no one paid much attention to them, although fishermen and divers must have known about them. There was no reason for anyone to think about man-made buildings or underwater cities.

Less than a mile from the shores of Bimini (an island in the Bahamas) is a series of long stone walls or roads. In recent years they have been examined many times by divers and archaeologists.

There are many other underwater formations around the Bahama Banks. Some are great stone circles that look like Stonehenge in England. They seem to form a path between the present-day islands. There are also circular walls around freshwater springs far below the surface. Archaeologists believe that the entire area of the Bahama Banks was above sea level before the last ice age.

Many pictures have been taken of the area from the air. The pictures show straight lines that intersect almost like the plans for a housing development. South of Bimini is a rectangle the size of a football field. Some archaeologists say these stones are merely beach rocks. But the rocks are arranged in neat rows. The stones are closely fitted and straight, and end in rounded corner

Underwater stones, found off the coast of Bimini, are arranged in a uniform pattern.

25

stones. The stone road does not follow the curve of the shore, but instead is a straight line. There are enormous flat stones, held up at their corners by pillar stones. Natural beach rocks do not appear in endless perfect rectangles and right angles. The arrangement of the stones closely resembles ancient tomb and temple structures around the world.

In February, 1969, an expedition sailed along the west coast of Bimini near a cliff called Paradise Point. The divers found what seemed to be a wide wall or roadbed that went north and south as far as they could

This is another aerial view of Bimini. Scientists have used photos taken from the air to locate underwater formations.

see. The rocks in the bed were huge and rectangular. On further study, the "bed" proved to be about seven hundred yards (640 m) long. The divers felt that this construction was man-made. The stones were fitted into a pavement pattern of right angles. After further dives, they thought the construction might be a seawall, a plaza, or the floor of a huge temple. Others thought it might be a seawall or dike on which a temple might have been constructed.

A former professor at Yale University felt the structure dated from eight to ten thousand years B.C. This

The mountains erupt in fire! The last hours of the city are shown in the movie, **Atlantis: The Lost Continent.**

was a geological era just before the Florida Straits were formed. It would also have been the last time that this part of the ocean floor could possibly have been above sea level.

All the experts who have seen the wall believe that it would never have been useful in any way as an underwater structure. Some experts believe that the wall may be even older than ten thousand years.

Two months after this expedition, an underwater expert returned and made a complete photographic study of the area.

It is difficult to know what the structure originally looked like. In 1926, a hurricane swept through the area. Many of the stones were taken to Miami to use in the reconstruction of piers and bridges.

Chapter 6

One theory today is that Atlantis was an island, not a continent, and that it was somewhere near Greece. One archaeologist believes that the Greek island of Thera, also called Santorini, was Atlantis. He believes that a tremendous volcanic explosion took place there around 1500 B.C. He also believes that Thera was once a circular island. It is now shaped like a crescent. The rest of the island exploded and disappeared under the Aegean Sea.

Another theory says that when the volcanic explosion happened, the island flipped over. What possibly was Atlantis is now buried deep under water. The sight of Santorini is so startling that this theory is easy to believe.

Santorini rises steeply out of the water, with layer after layer of red, black and white volcanic rock. A zig-zag path stretches up the cliff from a tiny port below. People usually ride mules up the path.

The archaeological digs on Thera have produced evidence of an advanced ancient culture. Many art treasures and beautiful houses have been found under 130 feet (40 m) of volcanic ash.

In 1967, a tunnel was dug through 160 feet (49 m) of rock. The tunnel revealed a town from the Bronze

Volcanic lightning probably occured during the destruction of Atlantis.

The island of Santorini rises steeply out of the ocean.

Out of the volcanic ash of Santorini, artifacts—like these jugs—have been found. Did this belong to an Atlantean?

Age (about 3500 B.C.) of some thirty thousand people. Two- and three-story buildings were found preserved by the ash from the exploding volcano. The buildings are located on fifty-foot (15 m) street fronts and still show traces of balconies. Frescoes on the buildings show men and birds, antelope and various plants. There are also frescoes of apes, an animal not pictured any-

Entire towns have been excavated from Santorini.

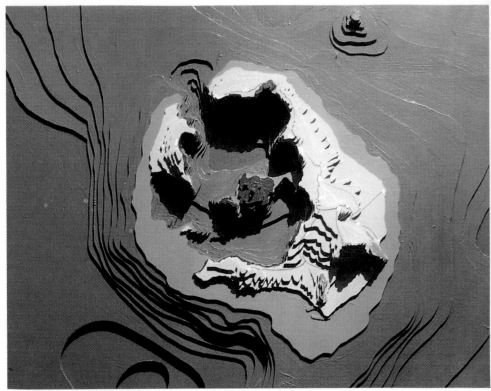
Shown in this model is the volcanic area of Santorini.

where else in that area.

No human remains have been found. This has led archaeologists to believe that the islanders must have been warned ahead of time that the volcano would explode.

In 1956, another great earthquake hit Santorini, and there still are active volcanic craters.

Chapter 7

Atlantis is called a legend for a number of reasons. The obvious one is that we're not certain anything is left of it. We can't see it with our own eyes. A second reason is that the story has been passed down through the years. The story was first spoken, not written. Legends tend to get changed in their tellings. The stories become exaggerated. Kings and leaders take on an aura of divine powers. They become known as gods or demi-gods.

The Greek myths state that the gods came down from the heavens and lived on high mountain tops. In reality, they were probably rulers who built their palaces and fortresses on high ground, making it easier to defend themselves against enemy attacks. When swirling mists and fogs hid the mountain tops from the view of the common people, the rulers began to take on a mystical quality. Many generations later, these rulers had been transformed through legends into gods and goddesses.

A Mexican myth talks about a ''great hand'' that seems to have been considered a god. The same figure is also found in Mayan mythology, where it is called ''the working hand.'' This great hand is identified with Atlantis in medieval legends. A map which dates from

Plato may have named Atlantis for the Greek god, Atlas. According to Greek myth, Atlas must hold the heavens on his shoulders forever.

This picture shows an undersea excavation project of the future.

1436 A.D. shows an island with an Italian name that translates as "the hand of Satan." This is tied to an old Italian romance which told of a great hand that rose every day from the sea and carried off a number of people into the ocean. This idea seems to be connected with the idea of earthquakes or giant tides.

There seems to be a worldwide chain of legends that

mention great upheavals of land. These may have been earthquakes. Our own familiar story of Noah's ark is repeated in almost every corner of the world, although with different characters. If there was a huge world disaster caused by earthquakes and volcanoes, it would have been followed by great floods. But would such a disaster have been powerful enough to sink an entire continent? And if it did, was it the continent of Atlantis?

Some scholars also believe that certain species of animals "remember" a lost land. In the thick seaweed of the Sargasso Sea in the North Atlantic Ocean, there is a deep underwater river. Eels from rivers in Europe and America swim there to mate.

Some birds that migrate from Europe to South America every year circle over a certain area in the Atlantic. Could they be looking for a resting place that no longer exists?

Some day we may find Atlantis, but for now it remains a mystery.

The lemmings of Norway swim out to the Atlantic Ocean in great masses, as if looking for a land that is no longer there. When they fail to find it, they circle aimlessly until they drown.

It seems likely that the next great archaeological digging will be done beneath the sea. With our modern research vessels, deep diving equipment and submarines, it is very possible that some day the remains of Atlantis will be found . . . if, in truth, it ever existed.

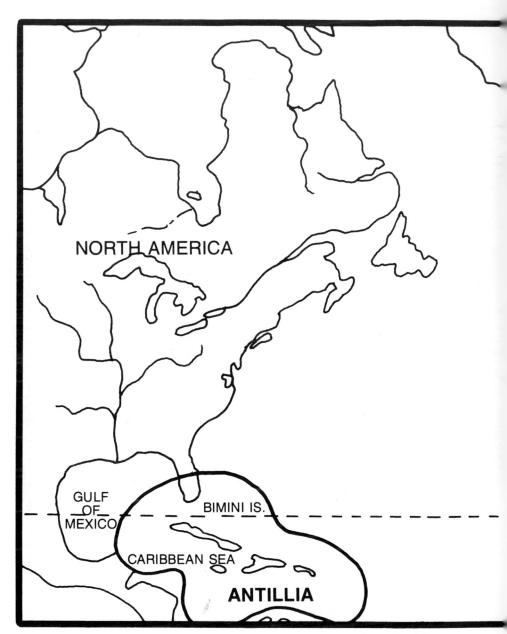

This map shows the possible locations of Atlantis, as described in this book.

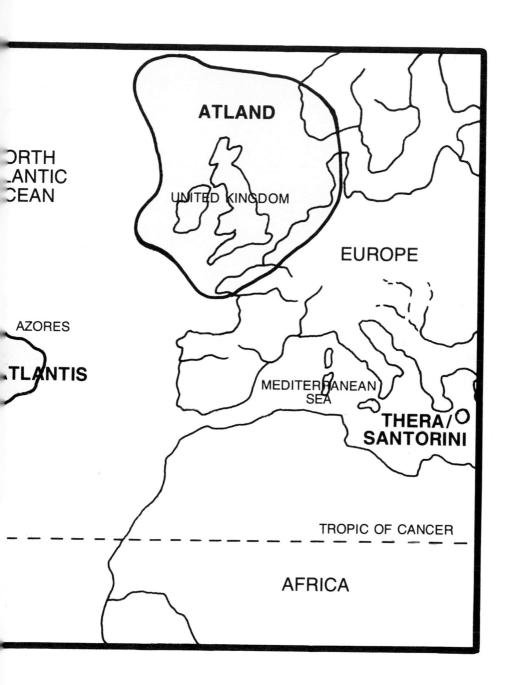

NORTH
ATLANTIC
OCEAN

ATLAND

UNITED KINGDOM

EUROPE

AZORES

ATLANTIS

MEDITERRANEAN
SEA

THERA/
SANTORINI

TROPIC OF CANCER

AFRICA

Map

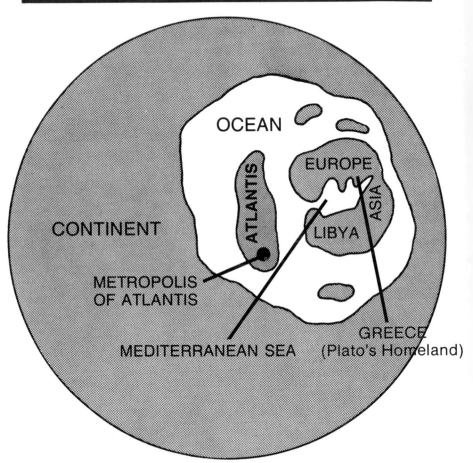

This was Plato's view of the world. He thought that the world known to him was surrounded by an ocean, which was in turn surrounded by a large continent. He felt that Atlantis was located somewhere in the ocean to the west of the Mediterranean Sea.

Glossary/Index

ARCHAEOLOGIST 23, 30, 36 — *Scientist who studies the remains of past human life.*

BERBER 8, 9 — *A North African tribe.*

CISTERN 14 — *Water tank.*

CITY-STATE 16 — *An independent political division consisting of a city and the surrounding area.*

COASTAL LOWLANDS 18 — *Low or level country near the sea.*

COLONIZATION 10 — *To establish communities in a new land.*

COMMERCE 10 — *The buying and selling of goods; trade.*

EXPEDITION 26, 29 — *A trip or outing, usually for the purpose of studying or exploring something.*

FRESCO 33 — *A painting on wet plaster.*

HIEROGLYPHIC 11 — *Writing in pictures.*

LEGEND 6, 13, 37, 38 — *A story that comes down to us from the past.*

LEMMING 43 — *A small furry animal with a short tail. Like mice and rats, lemmings have large front teeth which they use for gnawing.*

MYTH 4, 37, 38 — *A story that explains how things came into being, or that expresses the values of a people.*

PHILOSOPHER 4, 5 — *A scholar and student of truth.*

PROPHESY 17 — *A prediction of the future.*

PSYCHIC 17 — *A person sensitive to non-physical or supernatural forces.*

REFUGEES 8 — *People who leave their communities in order to find safety.*

SUBDUE 16 — *To bring under control.*

TRANCE 17 — *An intense state of mind. In a trance, a person is so completely absorbed in their thoughts that they are not aware of what's going on around them.*